Nature's Royal Tea Party

Written & Illustrated by Cheryl Kling

Dedicated To

My parents
Joan and George Kling for providing me with an idyllic childhood

Grama Barry, who introduced me to tea

and Steve Scopino for his unconditional love and support.

Thank you to my family and tea friends who have inspired and supported me.

Nature's Royal Tea Party copyright2009Cheryl Kling

ISBN: 978-0-615-29085-0
Library of Congress Control Number: 2009903882

Nature's Royalty are invited to the May Queen's tea party. The little Firefly is the messenger who delivers invitations to Queen Mum, Ladybug, Queen Bee, the Frog Prince, the Monarch Butterfly and others royal characters who prepare to celebrate with a secret guest of honor.

Printed in China by Everbest Printing Co. through Four Colour Imports, Ltd., Louisville, Kentucky

For more information contact:
Cheryl Kling
P.O.Box 372
Branford, CT 06405
cjkling@sbcglobal.net
www.cherylkling.com

As blossoms filled the tulip tree
The May Queen planned her Royal Tea.
Her forest friends were on her list
This party was not one to miss.
She sent the firefly to share
The invitations made with care.

She flew to find the garden space
And there was Queen Mum's friendly face.
"A Royal Tea," she bowed and said,
"With dewdrops dripped on honey bread?
I promise that I won't forget.
I will collect them freshly wet."

"I must suggest another guest,"
Her hands brushed through her petal crest,
I'd like to bring the Ladybug,"
Then thanked her with a gentle hug.
With that the firefly took off
To find the cousin of a moth.

She wasn't sure the reason why
Queen asked the Monarch Butterfly,
Her wings lined black on orange sheen
Like none the firefly had seen.
"Will Milkweed be set out for me?
I do require special tea."

She said that they must do their best
To cater to her odd request.
Though milkweed's poison to the others,
She said, "I'd rather have my druthers!"
"Oh, dear," the firefly began,
"I must be off to find Queen Anne."

She found a field of open space,
Queen Anne appeared all dressed in lace.
"I have some tea cups tell Queen May,
So perfect for her special day."
And tell her that I am so pleased
Her invitation includes weeds."

The firefly had tried her best,
But she was in the need of rest.
She sat upon a lily pad
And looking down she saw a tad.
"Please help me tadpole 'neath that log,
I'm looking for a Prince, a frog."

"That will be me," he said so slow,

"But you must give me time to grow.

The tea is on the first of May.

I will appear another way.

Right now all I can do is swim,

But that day you'll say "Look at him!"

The pond reflected clouds and sky.
A Damselfly came flitting by.
"Am I invited to the tea?
It's not a party without me!"
Her gold wings glistened in the sun,
"A May Tea can be so much fun!"

The firefly thought the damsel bold,
But "You are welcome," she was told.
A drop of water made a ring
Beside the regal Fisher King.
He had a brightly colored crown,
That did not match his saddened frown.

"Please tell, King Fisher, why you cry,"
Inquired little Firefly.
"I've caught a hook beneath my wing,"
He said. "I'm tangled up in string."
"I know it looks as if it's dire,"
She said, "but I can help you, Sire."

The Firefly lit up her flame,
Then singed the string and off it came.
King lifted up his injured wing,
The hook fell free, which made him sing.
"Please come enjoy the May Queen's Tea."
She then flew off to find Queen Bee.

She listened hard to hear the drone,
It meant the Queen was not alone.
"I do not do this work of mine.
The others do, it works out fine.
It gives me time to fuss and preen
And they just want to please their Queen."
Before the Firefly left the dome,
She said, "Please bring some honeycomb,
I heard it's used to sweeten tea
And that the best is yours, Queen Bee."
As darkness fell on all below
The Firefly could not light her glow.

She lay down by a moonlit stream
And fell into a pleasant dream.
The stars were bright against the sky.
They missed the little Firefly.
Then rising with a sleepy yawn,
The morning light announced the dawn.

The Firefly got all dressed up
And practiced how to hold a cup,
Imagining how it would be
With kings and queens all sipping tea.
Her clumsy curtsy made her smile,
But she would show she had good style.

The May Queen hinted she would greet
A special guest for all to meet.
She said she was a rising star,
They'd come to see her from afar.
Drums and flutes announced the day
And helped the guests to find their way.

Beneath the awning of a tree,
The May Queen sat to host her tea.
The water in the copper kettles
Was boiled for tea of herbs and petals.
She poured it in a China pot,
Then into cups, while it was hot.

The teacups were Queen Anne's to share,
Her flowered lace was everywhere.

The Frog Prince now with different traits,
Used waterlily pads as plates.
He wore a simple crown shaped hat,
Upon a toad stool, there he sat.

Cookies shaped like butterflies
Had stained glass wings from colored dyes.
The Monarch Butterfly flew low,
Admiring how she looked in dough.
Melon fish in hues of gold
Were in King Fisher's salad mold.

The Damselfly just loved to chat,
She flitted round and never sat.
Queen Mum had gathered morning dew
For something, but she had no clue.
"Oh, yes," alas she did recall,
"For dew drop sandwiches for all."

The Ladybug was with her too.
She brought some Jasmine tea to brew.
Sweet honey cakes and honey pie,
And honey pots were filled quite high.
The Queen Bee entered on her throne
It would save time had she just flown.

The Royalty had dressed their best
In honor of the mystery guest.
The May Queen planned activities,
Maypoles, leap frog, swings in trees,
A quest to fly the highest kite,
A special light show for that night.

The guest arrived for all to greet.
Surprised, they led her to her seat.
A truer friend no one could buy.
They honored their friend Firefly.
"I'm pleased to have your company,
I toast you with my cup of tea."

The afternoon grew into night,
Small Firefly cast lots of light.
A crown of stars enhanced her glow,
She was so pleased, she let it show.
As May Queen passed round Lemon Tarts,
A sense of joy filled all their hearts.